GENTE DE LAS FUERZAS ARMADAS DE EE.UU./PEOPLE OF THE U.S. ARMED FORCES

DE LA FUERZA AÉREA DE EE.UU.

OF THE U.S. AIR FORCE

por/by Lisa M. Bolt Simons

Editora consultora/Consulting Editor: Gail Saunders-Smith, PhD

Consultor/Consultant: Raymond L. Puffer, PhD
Historiador, Ret./Historian, Ret.
Edwards Air Force Base History Office

CAPSTONE PRESS
a capstone imprint

Pebble Plus is published by Capstone Press,
151 Good Counsel Drive, P.O. Box 669, Mankato, Minnesota 56002.
www.capstonepub.com

Books published by Capstone Press are manufactured with paper
containing at least 10 percent post-consumer waste.

Library of Congress Cataloging-in-Publication Data
Simons, Lisa M. B., 1969–
 [Airmen of the U.S. Air Force. Spanish & English]
 Airmen de la Fuerza Aérea de EE.UU. / por Lisa M. Bolt Simons =
  Airmen of the U.S. Air Force / by Lisa M. Bolt Simons.
  p. cm.—(Pebble Plus bilingüe. Gente de las fuerzas armadas de EE.UU. =
Pebble Plus bilingual. People of the armed forces)
 Includes index.
  ISBN 978-1-4296-6115-7 (library binding)
 1. United States. Air Force—Juvenile literature. I. Title. II. Title: Aimen de la Fuerza Aérea de Estados Unidos.
III. Title: Airmen of the U.S. Air Force. IV. Title: Airmen of the United States Air Force.
UG633.S49617 2011
358.4'1330973—dc22   2010041505

Editorial Credits
Gillia Olson, editor; Strictly Spanish, translation services; Renée T. Doyle, designer; Danielle Ceminsky,
    bilingual book designer; Laura Manthe, production specialist

Photo Credits
Capstone Press/Gary Sundermeyer, 21
DVIC/Sgt Olan A. Owens, 15
Getty Images Inc./Joe McNally, 9
Renée Doyle, 7
SuperStock, Inc./StockTrek, cover
U.S. Air Force photo, 17; by Master Sgt. Andy Dunaway, 5; by Master Sgt. Val Gempis, 11; by Randy Rubattino, 13;
    by Tech Sgt. Howard Blair, 10; by Tech Sgt. Chance Babin, 19

Artistic Effects
iStockphoto/luoman (radar screen), cover, 1, 24
Shutterstock/Jamey Ekins (cockpit view), 22–23; Shutterstock/The Labor Shed (control panel), 2, 24

Note to Parents and Teachers

The Gente de las Fuerzas Armadas de EE.UU./People of the U.S. Armed Forces series supports
national science standards related to science, technology, and society. This book describes and
illustrates airmen of the U.S. Air Force in both English and Spanish. The images support early
readers in understanding the text. The repetition of words and phrases helps early readers learn
new words. This book also introduces early readers to subject-specific vocabulary words, which
are defined in the Glossary section. Early readers may need assistance to read some words and
to use the Table of Contents, Glossary, Internet Sites, and Index sections of the book.

Printed in the United States of America in North Mankato, Minnesota.
022011   006080R

Table of Contents

Tabla de contenidos

Joining the Air Force

Men and women join
the United States Air Force
to protect the country.
They defend the skies
and space.

Unirse a la Fuerza Aérea

Mujeres y hombres se unen a la
Fuerza Aérea de Estados Unidos
para proteger al país. Ellos
defienden los cielos y el espacio.

4

Recruits go to basic training
in Texas for eight weeks.
They exercise and study.
They learn to march
and to shoot.

Los reclutas reciben entrenamiento
básico en Texas durante ocho
semanas. Ellos hacen ejercicios
y estudian. Ellos aprenden a
marchar y a disparar.

Job Training

After basic training, recruits are called airmen. Then, they train for their jobs. Crew chiefs fix planes, like the F-22 Raptor.

Entrenamiento para el trabajo

Después del entrenamiento básico, los reclutas son llamados *airmen*. Luego ellos se entrenan para sus trabajos. Los jefes de equipo reparan aviones, como el F-22 Raptor.

Some airmen become pilots.
They fly planes. Pilots use the C-130
Hercules to carry airmen and supplies.

Algunos *airmen* se vuelven pilotos.
Ellos pilotean aviones. Los pilotos
usan el C-130 Hercules para
transportar *airmen* y suministros.

Some airmen control radar.

They use radar to watch

the sky and space.

Algunos *airmen* controlan el radar.

Ellos usan el radar para vigilar

el cielo y el espacio.

Living on Base

Most airmen live on bases.

Bases have homes, stores,

and hospitals for airmen

and their families.

Vivir en la base

La mayoría de los *airmen* viven

en bases. Las bases tienen casas,

tiendas y hospitales para los

airmen y sus familias.

15

Bases are in the United States
and around the world. Airmen
often move to another base
every four years.

Las bases están en Estados Unidos
y en todo el mundo. Los *airmen*
a menudo se mudan a otra base
cada cuatro años.

Serving the Country

Most airmen serve for four or six years. Career airmen stay in the Air Force for 20 years or more.

Servir al país

La mayoría de los *airmen* sirve de cuatro a seis años. Los *airmen* de carrera permanecen en la Fuerza Aérea durante 20 años o más.

After serving, airmen leave the Air Force to be civilians. Some go to college. Others use their skills and training to find jobs.

Después del servicio, los *airmen* dejan la Fuerza Aérea para ser civiles. Algunos van a la universidad. Otros usan sus destrezas y entrenamiento para buscar trabajos.

Glossary

base—an area run by the military where people serving in the military live and military supplies are stored

basic training—the first training period for people who join the military

civilian—a person who is not in the military

crew chief—a person who fixes airplanes and other machines in the Air Force

radar—equipment that uses radio waves to find and guide objects

recruit—a person who has just joined the military

Internet Sites

FactHound offers a safe, fun way to find Internet sites related to this book. All of the sites on FactHound have been researched by our staff.

Here's all you do:

Visit *www.facthound.com*

Type in this code: 9781429661157

Super-cool stuff!

Check out projects, games and lots more at
www.capstonekids.com

Glosario

la base—un área administrada por las Fuerzas Armadas donde vive la gente en servicio y donde se almacenan los suministros militares

civil—una persona que no está en las Fuerzas Armadas

el entrenamiento básico—el primer período de entrenamiento para las personas que se unen a las Fuerzas Armadas

el jefe de equipo—una persona que repara aviones y otras máquinas en la Fuerza Aérea

el radar—equipamiento que usa ondas de radio para buscar y guiar objetos

el recluta—una persona que recién se unió a las Fuerzas Armadas

Sitios de Internet

FactHound brinda una forma segura y divertida de encontrar sitios de Internet relacionados con este libro. Todos los sitios en FactHound han sido investigados por nuestro personal.

Esto es todo lo que tienes que hacer:

Visita *www.facthound.com*

Ingresa este código: 9781429661157

 ¡Algo súper divertido! Hay proyectos, juegos y mucho más en www.capstonekids.com

23

Index

Índice